The Balanced Christian Life

Michael Penny

A series of five studies based on Ephesians

Exploring ...

The blessings Christians have in Christ

and

Explaining ...

The practical Christian life

which should follow.

ISBN: 978-1-78364-485-8

The Open Bible Trust
Fordland Mount, Upper Basildon,
Reading, RG8 8LU, UK.

www.obt.org.uk

The Balanced Christian Life

Contents

****

Introduction

The Christian life is one of *balance.*

Doctrine v Practice

The *doctrine* **must** come first, but the *practice* **must** follow. This is shown very much in Paul's letter to the Ephesians, where he tells the Christians what their *blessings* are in Christ first, and then tells them what their *response* should be.

Blessings first, then our response

In fact Ephesians is a letter all about *balance.* By and large, the first three chapters are about doctrine and blessings, and the last three about practice. The whole letter is balanced on the word 'Therefore' in Ephesians 4:1.

"I *therefore,* the prisoner of the Lord, beseech you that you walk worthy of the vocation wherewith you are called." (*KJV*)

"As a prisoner for the Lord, *then* (*therefore*), I urge you to live a life worthy of the calling you have received." *(NIV)*

Whenever you see the word "therefore" you need always ask, "What is it there for?"

So it is imperative that Christians understand some of the *doctrine,* and know some of the *blessings*, before they are asked to *respond* in their *practice.*

Background to Ephesians

Ephesians was written while Paul was in prison in Rome about AD 64 (see Acts 28:30). It is the most impersonal of Paul's letters because, in fact, it is a general letter to many churches. The reference to Ephesus in the opening is not in the best ancient manuscripts. That being the case, this letter is then:

"To the saints and faithful in Christ Jesus *everywhere*."

The doctrine of the letter supports this view because it contains the highest church truth, but says nothing about church order. The church in this letter is the true church, "the body of Christ". It is not the local church, but the universal church of all Christians. It is not the physical church, but the spiritual one.

Essentially there are three lines of teaching.

1. The believer's exalted position through grace - the doctrine, the blessings.
2. Teaching concerning the church, the body of Christ.
3. The Christian walk; the worthy life - the response, the practice.

In these studies we shall be concentrating on the first and third.

The Aim of this book

These studies have been used by many people privately, but they have also been used with Lent groups and house groups, and with church Bible Studies and on Christian holidays and retreats. I am most grateful for the comments and criticisms received which have significantly improved and altered these studies. My prayer is that they will enable more Christians to appreciate more deeply some of the blessings we have in Christ, and that this will then motivate us to live a life more worthy of the name 'Christian'.

How to use this book – Personal Study or Group Discussion

Each study is a mixture of doctrine or blessing. The blessings are focused upon and then follows questions or taasks dealing with what should be the practical response to that particular blessing.

When the reader is asked 'to fill in the blank spaces' or complete some task, please try to think what the missing words are or the answers to the task. The missing words or suggested answers and comments come straight afterwards, and we pray some of the comments will be thought provoking and m ay lead to opening up discussion if this is being studied in a group. The desire is that this will lead to a deeper Bible understanding of the Bible.

If this book is being used for a group study the answers, then many of the questions can be discussed and answered compared before going on to the answers supplied in the book.

The Balanced Christian Life

The Christian life is one of balance.

A balance between …

Doctrine v Practice

or
Blessings (first)

And then our response
Or

"Therefore" (Ephesians 4:1; *KJV*)

"Then" (Ephesians 4:1; *NIV*)

I, *therefore*, the prisoner of the Lord,
beseech you that you walk worthy of the vocation
wherewith you are called.

As a prisoner for the Lord, *then,*
I urge you to live a life worthy of the calling
you have received.

Whenever you see THEREFORE,

you always ask what is it _ _ _ _ _   _ _ _

Study 1.
Praise

Ephesians 1:1

1. Paul, an apostle of Christ Jesus by the will of God, to the saints in Ephesus, the faithful in Christ Jesus:

Question: What is an "apostle"?

This comes from the Greek word *apostolos*, and means "one who has been sent". The *apostles* of the Bible were sent by Christ. Peter, James, John and the rest of the Twelve were sent by Christ only to the Jews. Paul was sent by Christ to the Gentiles, as well as the Jews.

Question: Who is a "saint"?

This word was hi-jacked many years ago to apply only to super-Christians. However, all Christians are saints. The word means 'holy ones', and the idea behind 'holy' is to be 'separate', to be different. There are two sides to holiness. All Christians are holy because when they believe in Christ as their Saviour, God separates them to Himself; this makes them different. However, He now wants them to separate themselves from the ways of the world; i.e. to live a different, holy life.

Question: Who are "faithful?"

This word means to be trusted, to be reliable. Whereas all the Christians are holy, not all are faithful. But to be faithful does not mean to be 100% reliable all of the time. The Bible is very clear in describing the failings of many of the leading, faithful, children of God.

Ephesians 1:2

2. Grace and peace to you from God our Father and the Lord Jesus Christ.

Question: What is "grace"?

Grace has been termed 'unmerited favour'; Christians get what they do *not* deserve because God is a God of grace.

Question: What is "peace"?

We usually refer to peace as the absence of war, or being free from trouble. However, the Greek word is very positive. It corresponds to the total-wellbeing of the person. It wants everything for man's highest good that can come from God.

Ephesians 1:3
Fill in the blanks below:

_ _ _ _ _ _ be to the God and Father of our Lord Jesus Christ, who has _ _ _ _ _ _ _ us in the heavenly realms with every spiritual _ _ _ _ _ _ _ in Christ.

However, if we translated the Greek consistently it would read:

PRAISE be to the God and Father of our Lord Jesus Christ, who has **PRAISED** us in heavenly realms with every spiritual **PRAISE** in Christ.

You will note that we have, basically, put in the same word, 'praise' in all three places. This is because in the Greek all the words are derivatives of *eulogia*, which means to praise, to eulogise over, to speak well of, to praise. So we should eulogise over, or praise God, because He eulogises over us; i.e. He praises us.

Question: How does this work? What does God say?

To answer these questions consider the example of Job.

Question: What did God say about Job?
Let's look at Job 1:8.
Fill in the blanks below:

Then the LORD said to Satan. "Have you considered my servant Job? There is no one on earth _ _ _ _ him; he is _ _ _ _ _ _ _ _ _ and _ _ _ _ _ _ _, a man who _ _ _ _ _ God and shuns _ _ _ _."

> Then the Lord said to Satan, "Have you considered my servant Job? There is no one on earth **like** him; he is **blameless** and **upright**, a man who **fears** God and shuns **evil**."

Here is God praising, speaking well of, eulogising over Job.

Question: What does it mean to *FEAR* God?

It does not mean to be afraid of God; rather it means to be in 'awe' of God. He is an awesome God. (If doing this with a group, discuss 'awe'.)

Let's look at Job 2:3
Fill in the blanks:

Then the LORD said to Satan, "Have you considered my servant Job? There is no one on earth _ _ _ _ him; he is _ _ _ _ _ _ _ _ _ and _ _ _ _ _ _ _, a man who _ _ _ _ _ God and shuns _ _ _ _. And he still _ _ _ _ _ _ _ _ _ his _ _ _ _ _ _ _ _, though you incited me against him to ruin him without any reason."

> Then the Lord said to Satan, "Have you considered my servant Job? There is no one on earth **like** him; he is **blameless** and **upright**, a man who **fears** God and shuns **evil**. And he still **maintains** his **integrity**, though you incited me against him to ruin him without any reason."

Note: We should maintain our Christian integrity no matter what befalls us.

Question: What did Christ say about John the Baptist?

Let's look at Luke 7:28.
Fill in the blanks.

I tell you, among those born of women there is no one _ _ _ _ _ _ _ than John; yet the one who is least in the kingdom of God is _ _ _ _ _ _ _ than he.

> "I tell you among those born of women there is no one **greater** than John; yet the one who is least in the kingdom of God is **greater** than he."

We might feel unworthy, and that God might seldom, if ever, praise us, but remember earthly parents often eulogise over their children so it should not surprise us that God does the same with His children. Jesus said this of John, just **after** John had started doubting whether or not Jesus was the Messiah. Read *NIV* Luke 7:18-23.

> John's disciples told him about all these things. Calling two of them, he sent them to the Lord to ask, "Are you the one who is to come, or should we expect someone else?" When the men came to Jesus, they said, "John the Baptist sent us to you to ask, 'Are you the one who is to come, or should we expect someone else?'" At that very time Jesus cured many who had diseases, sicknesses and evil spirits, and gave sight to many who were blind. So he replied to the messengers, "Go back and report to John what you have seen and heard: The blind receive sight, the lame walk, those who have leprosy are cleansed, the deaf hear, the dead are raised, and the good news is proclaimed to the poor. Blessed is anyone who does not stumble on account of me."

Question: What sort of people will be *LEAST* in the kingdom of God?

Think about this question but if in a group, have a general discussion on this question.

In Christ's day the 'least' would have been the sinners, tax collectors, prostitutes who had put their faith in Christ.

Question: Who do people consider to be the 'least' Christians in society today?

TASK!
Write down three things God could *praise* you for.
Write down three things God could *criticise* you for.

Praises

1.

2

3.

Criticisms

1.

2.

3.

If in a group, they can keep their answers confidential, if they wish, or they can share some of them afterwards.

The group may like to share some of the things they think God will praise them for. After some discussion, they may be willing to share some of the things they think God will criticise them for.

Question: Are we correct in our answers?

We may well be right in our assessment of what God praises us for, but what about the criticisms?

Let's look at Ephesians 1:4-5.
Fill in the blanks.

For he [God] chose us in him before the creation of the world to be _ _ _ _ and _ _ _ _ _ _ _ _ _ in his sight. In love he predestined us to be _ _ _ _ _ _ _ as his _ _ _ _ through Jesus Christ, in accordance with his pleasure and will.

> For he [God] chose us in him before the creation of the world to be **holy** and **blameless** in his sight. In love he predestined us to be **adopted** as his **sons** through Jesus Christ, in accordance with his pleasure and will.

Thus in God's sight we are **holy** and **blameless**. This is due to the fact that Christ has taken our sins away from us. All this is, as Ephesians 1:6 puts it:

> … to the praise of his glorious grace, which he has freely given us in the One he loves.

Perhaps we are beginning to understand 'grace' just a little more deeply: unmerited favour. We don't merit being 'holy and blameless' in God's sight and certainly we don't deserve this from God, but this is what we get.

Note 1: '*adopted* sons', under the Greek Law of that time, could not be disinherited.

Note 2: Christians are "holy and blameless in His [God's] sight". That does not mean that we actually are blameless or sinless, but we are "in His [God's] sight". That is because we are "in Christ" and God looks on us "in Christ". He sees us "through Christ". He looks on us through rose coloured glasses, and the red in those glasses is the precious blood of Christ which He shed on Calvary's cross.

Questions: How did God *use* to look on us? How does He look on us *now*?

Let's look at Colossians 1:21-22.
Fill in the blanks.

Question: How did God use to look on us?

ONCE YOU WERE _ _ _ _ _ _ _ _ _ from _ _ _ and were
_ _ _ _ _ _ _ in your minds because of your _ _ _ _ behaviour.

> Once you were **alienated** from **God** and were **enemies** in your
> minds because of your **evil** behaviour.

Question: How does He look on us *now*?

BUT NOW HE [God] has _ _ _ _ _ _ _ _ _ _ you by Christ's
physical body through death to present you _ _ _ _ in
_ _ _ _ _ _ _ _, without _ _ _ _ _ _ _ and free from
_ _ _ _ _ _ _ _ _.

> But now he has **reconciled** you by Christ's physical body
> through death to present you **holy** in **his sight** without **blemish**
> and free from **accusation**.

Note again that this is "in His sight".

Question: Is this true of *ALL* Christians?

Let's look at Ephesians 5:25-27.
Fill in the blanks.

Christ loved the church [i.e. the people, not the building] and gave
himself up for her to make her _ _ _ _, _ _ _ _ _ _ _ _ _ _ her by the
washing with water through the word, and to present her to himself
as a _ _ _ _ _ _ _ church, without _ _ _ _ _ or _ _ _ _ _ _ _ or any
other _ _ _ _ _ _ _, but _ _ _ _ and _ _ _ _ _ _ _ _ _.

Christ loved the church and gave himself up for her to make her **holy, cleansing** her by the washing with water through the word, and to present her to himself as a **radiant** church, without **stain** or **wrinkle** or any other **blemish**, but **holy** and **blameless.**

Thus, the church, i.e. all Christians, have been cleansed and are holy. They are radiant, without stain or wrinkle, or any other blemish. They are holy and blameless.

Question 1*: Could* **we write down three things God could** *criticise* **us for?**

Answer 1: We could all write down many more than three.

Question 2: *Should* **we write down three things God could** *criticise* **us for?**

Answer 2: No! Because to do so, shows we do not understand the character of our heavenly Father. He does not criticise us for our sins. He knows we are sinners. That is why He sent His Son. Christ came and died so that our sins could be removed.

Psalm 103:10-12
Fill in the blanks.

He [God] does not _ _ _ _ _ us as our _ _ _ _ deserve or _ _ _ _ _ us according to our _ _ _ _ _ _ _ _ _ _. For as high as the heavens are above the earth, so great is his _ _ _ _ for those who *fear* him; as far as the _ _ _ _ is from the _ _ _ _, so far as he removed our _ _ _ _ _ _ _ _ _ _ _ _ _ from us.

He [God] does not **treat** us as our **sins** deserve or **repay** us according to our **iniquities**. For as high as the heavens are above the earth, so great is his **love** for those who fear him; as far as the **east** is from the **west**, so far has he removed our **transgressions** from us.

Christ came so that God could actively forget sins. Speaking of Israel He says:

Jeremiah 31:34

Fill in the blanks.

"No longer will a man teach his neighbour, or a man his brother, saying 'Know the LORD,' because they will all know me, from the least of them to the greatest," declares the LORD. "For I will
_ _ _ _ _ _ _ their wickedness and will _ _ _ _ _ _ _ _ their sins no more."

> "No longer will a man teach his neighbour, or a man his brother, saying, 'Know the Lord,' because they will all know me, from the least of them to the greatest," declares the Lord. "For I will **forgive** their wickedness and will **remember** their sins no more."

God is the only person who can choose to purposely forget.

**So our sins are forgiven
and our sins are forgotten**

And we also must realise that we should not abuse such grace and forgiveness, and think that we can sin as much as we like, as some of the Christians in Rome did; see Romans 6:1-2.

**Grace gives us liberty to serve,
and ensures forgiveness when we slip.
It does not give us license to sin.**

BIG Question: SO…what should our response be to the fact that we are saved and that God praises us, speaks well of us, eulogises over us?

Our general orders come from: Ephesians 2:8-10:
Fill in the blanks.

For it is by grace you have been save, through faith – and this is not from yourselves, it is the gift of God – not by works, so that no one can boast. For we are God's workmanship, *created in Christ Jesus _ _ _ _ _ _ _ _ _ _ _ _ _*, which God prepared in advance for us to do.

> For it is by grace you have been saved, through faith – and this not from yourselves, it is the gift of God – not by works, so that no one can boast. For we are God's workmanship, created in Christ Jesus **to do good works**, which God prepared in advance for us to do.

Question: So … what should those good works be?

Ephesians 4:1-3 sets the tone.

> As a prisoner for the Lord, then, I urge you to live a life worthy of the calling you have received.

Question: What do we have to do to live a worthy life?

> Be completely humble and gentle;
> be patient, bearing with one another in love.

Question: How can we do that?

Make every effort to keep the unity of the Spirit
through the bond of peace.

Question: What do we have to do?

Ephesians 4:29-5:2 gives some good works which are relevant to
the blessings we have been considering. We shall look at it in
sections.

Ephesians 4:29-30.
Fill in the blanks.

Do not let any unwholesome _ _ _ _ come out of your mouths, but
only what is _ _ _ _ _ _ _ for building others up according to their
_ _ _ _ _, that it may _ _ _ _ _ _ _ those who listen.

And do not _ _ _ _ _ _ the Holy Spirit of God, with whom you were
sealed for the day of redemption.

> Do not let any unwholesome **talk** come out of your mouths, but
> only what is **helpful** for building others up according to their
> **needs**, that it may **benefit** those who listen. And do not **grieve**
> the Holy Spirit of God, with whom you were sealed for the day
> of redemption.

Thus if God speaks well of us, praises us, eulogises over us,
unwholesome talk should not come out of our mouths. Rather what
we say should be helpful in building up others, meeting their needs,
and benefiting all who listen. Also notice that:

> **Although God forgives and forgets our sins,**
> **and, in Christ, He sees us as holy and blameless,**
> **and without spot or blemish …**
>
> **our sins grieve Him.**

Ephesians 4:31
Fill in the blanks.

Get rid of all _ _ _ _ _ _ _ _ _ _, _ _ _ _ and _ _ _ _ _,
_ _ _ _ _ _ _ _ and _ _ _ _ _ _ _, along with every form of
_ _ _ _ _ _.

Get rid of all **bitterness**, **rage** and **anger**, **brawling** and **slander**, along with every form of **malice**.

Ephesians 4:32
Fill in the blanks.

Be _ _ _ _ and _ _ _ _ _ _ _ _ _ _ _ _ _ _ _ to one another,
_ _ _ _ _ _ _ _ _ each other, just as in Christ God _ _ _ _ _ _ _ you.

Be **kind** and **compassionate** to one another, **forgiving** each other, just as in Christ God **forgave** you.

Again, if God praises us, speaks well of us, and eulogises over us, there should be no bitterness, rage, anger, slander or malice in what we say of others, and especially of what we say of other Christians. Our tongues so often let us down, as James says.

With the tongue we praise our Lord and Father, and with it we curse men, who have been made in God's likeness. Out of the same mouth come praise and cursing. My brothers this should not be. (James 3:9-10)

God praises us … **all** of us. Not only should we praise God, we should also praise each other.

God has not only forgiven us our sins, but also has forgotten them. We do not have the capacity to actively forget, but we do have the capacity to forgive, and we should forgive because we have been forgiven.

Ephesians 5:1-2
Fill in the blanks.

Be _ _ _ _ _ _ _ _ _ of God, therefore, as dearly _ _ _ _ _ children and live a _ _ _ _ of love, just as Christ _ _ _ _ _ us and gave himself up for us as a fragrant offering and sacrifice to God.

> Be **imitators** of God, therefore, as dearly **loved** children and live a **life** of love, just as Christ **loved** us and gave himself up for us as a fragrant offering and sacrifice to God.

We can be imitators of God.

Getting the balance right
Blessings and response

God speaks well of us,
we can imitate him by speaking well of others.

He praises us,
we can imitate Him by praising others.

He forgives us,
we can imitate Him by forgiving others.

He gave His Son,
we can imitate Him by giving to others.

We should give money to the church and charities, but what can we give to individuals, many of whom are not short of money and are in no need of material items? Time, compassion, sympathy, may be three things.

Question: What else can we give?

Think about answers to this last question. If in a group, please discuss the question.

Study 2.
Riches

Ephesians 1:5-8

Fill in the blanks.

He [God] predestined us to be _ _ _ _ _ _ _ as his _ _ _ _ through
Jesus Christ, in accordance with his _ _ _ _ _ _ _ _ and will – to the
praise of his glorious grace, which he has freely given us in the One
he loves. In him we have _ _ _ _ _ _ _ _ _ _ through his blood, the
_ _ _ _ _ _ _ _ _ _ of sins, in accordance with the _ _ _ _ _ _ of
God's grace that he _ _ _ _ _ _ _ _ on us with all wisdom and
understanding.

> He [God] [predestined is to be **adopted** as his **sons** through
> Jesus Christ, in accordance with his **pleasure** and will – to the
> praise of his glorious grace, which he has freely given us in the
> One he loves. In him we have **redemption** through his blood,
> the **forgiveness** of sins, in accordance with the *riches* of God's
> grace, that he **lavished** on us with all wisdom and
> understanding.

**Question: Which is better: to be a 'real' child or an 'adopted'
child?**

This letter was sent to the Greek/Roman world of Paul's day.
There, at that time, a natural son could be disinherited, but an
adopted son could not. The inheritance was guaranteed; see
Ephesians 1:14.

Question: What does 'sin' mean?

In Romans 3:23 Paul wrote, "all have sinned and *fall short* of the glory of God." So to sin means to fall short of the mark. The Christian's mark is Jesus Christ and as we fall short of Him and His standards; we all sin. One of the main reasons we fall short, we sin, is because we put ourselves and what we want at the centre of our lives, rather than God and others. So it has been said that since the middle letter of 'sin' is 'I':

Sin has 'I' in th933e centre

As we live in the 'me' generation, perhaps we should say that sin has 'me' in the centre.

Question: What does 'redemption' mean?

This word is little used in our society. The main usage is when someone 'redeems' their mortgage; i.e. they pay it off early and so 'buy back' the title deeds of their house from the bank. In earlier years people used pawn shops, and could 'redeem' the article they left as surety by paying back the loan with interest. In the same way, Christ's death has redeemed us and …

Fill in the blanks.

We have been _ _ _ _ _ _ back from _ _ _ and _ _ _ _ _.

We have been **BOUGHT** back from **SIN** and **DEATH**.

Question: What does 'forgiveness' mean?

When God forgives our sins, He also forgets them. When we have been redeemed we are also forgiven and we are justified, and so forgiveness and justification mean:

Justified: Just-as-if-I'd never _ _ _ _ _ _.

Justified: just-as-if-I'd never **SINNED**

Question: What does 'lavished' mean?

The purpose of this question is to make people realise that God does not begrudgingly forgive us. He has 'lavished' on us the 'riches' of His grace.

A prayer for three things: Ephesians 1:18-19
Fill in the blanks.

I pray also that the eyes of your heart may be enlightened in order that you may know …

1. the _ _ _ _ to which he has called you,
2. the _ _ _ _ _ _ of his glorious inheritance in the saints,
3. and his incomparably great _ _ _ _ _ for us who believe.

I pray also that the eyes of your heart may be enlightened in order that you may know …

1. the **hope** to which he has called you,
2. the **riches** of his glorious inheritance in the saints,
3. and his incomparably great **power** for us who believe.

Question: What does 'hope' mean?

When we use the word 'hope' in English, there is usually an element of doubt attached to it. For example, if invited somewhere we may reply, "I hope to come, I will let you know for sure."

However, this is not the case with the Greek word for hope, *elpis*: it means "favourable and confident expectation." Paul puts it this way in Hebrews 11:1:

> Now faith is being sure of what we hope for and certain of what we do not see.

Here, together with the word 'hope' we have 'sure' and 'certain'. And note what is said earlier about the inheritance, which is our hope; it is guaranteed; Ephesians 1:14.

Question: What does 'grace' mean?

We asked a similar question in Study 1, but it is worth repeating and consolidating as many Christians either do not understand 'grace' or lack confidence that they are worthy of God's grace. The fact is that none of us are 'worthy' of God's grace, and 'worthiness' has nothing to do with grace. Grace is 'unmerited favour' and so Christians get what they do **not** deserve (e.g. forgiveness and eternal life) because God is a God of grace.

An acronym for 'grace'.
Fill in the blanks.

G _ _ _ ' _

R _ _ _ _ _ _

A _ _

C _ _ _ _ _ _ ' _

E _ _ _ _ _ _

One acronym which fits the blanks is:

God's Riches At Christ's Expense

Another acronym is:

Gift's Received At Christ's Expense

Question: What 'gifts' we do have, or we will have, because Christ died for us?

Some of the 'gifts we have are forgiveness, salvation, son ship, eternal life, righteousness in eternal life, a new body in eternal life.

Ephesians 2:4-5
Fill in the blanks.

But because of his great _ _ _ _ for us, God, who is rich in _ _ _ _ , made us alive with Christ even when we were dead in transgression - it is by grace you have been saved.

> But because of His great **love** for us, God, who is rich in **mercy**, made us alive with Christ even when we were dead in **transgressions** - it is by grace you have been saved.

Notice again the richness of the language. It is not simply 'God's love but 'God's **great** love'. It is not simply 'mercy' but God 'is **rich** in mercy'. Such is our Heavenly Father.

Question: What is God going to do with us in eternal life?

Ephesians 2:6-7
Fill in the blanks.

And God raised us up with Christ and seated us with him in the heavenly realms in Christ Jesus, in order that in the coming ages he might show the _ _ _ _ _ _ _ _ _ _ _ _   _ _ _ _ _ _ of his grace, expressed in his kindness to us in Christ Jesus.

> And God raised us up with Christ and seated us with him in heavenly realms in Christ Jesus, in order that in the coming ages he might show the **incomparable riches** of his grace expressed in his kindness to us in Christ Jesus.

This is not only grace, but we are to have **riches** of His grace. But more than that!

However, it is not just an issue of the riches of His grace; we have the **incomparable** riches of his grace. But more than that!

It is going to take God **coming ages** to show us those incomparable riches of His grace. No wonder Paul writes …

> No eye has seen, no ear has heard, no mind has conceived what God has prepared for those who love him. (1 Corinthians 2:9)

Can we possibly conceive what it means by "the unsearchable riches of His grace"? No! But this is what God is going to do with us in eternal life.

Question: What was Paul's job?

Ephesians 3:8
Fill in the blanks.

Although I am less than the least of all God's people, this grace was given me: to preach to the Gentiles the _ _ _ _ _ _ _ _ _ _ _ _ _ _ _ _ _ of Christ.

Although I am less than the least of all God's people, this grace was given me: to preach to the Gentiles the **unsearchable riches** of Christ.

Question: What is our job?

Perhaps our job is the same as Paul's. However, to be able to do it, we must know something about those 'unsearchable riches'. Here are two other aspects of the work of a Christian.

Always be prepared to give an answer to everyone who asks you to give the reason for the hope that you have. (1 Peter 3:15)

To be able to do the first we must know and understand our 'hope'. See Colossians 4:6 for another aspect of the work of a Christian.

Another prayer: Ephesians 3:16-17
Fill in the blanks.

I pray that out of his glorious _ _ _ _ _ _ he [God] may strengthen you with power through his Spirit in your inner being *so that* Christ may dwell in your hearts through faith.

I pray that out of his glorious **riches** he may strengthen you with power through His Spirit in your inner being, so that Christ may dwell in your hearts through faith.

Again note it is not simply 'riches' but **glorious** riches'. And here God will strengthen us with power in our inner being, so that Christ will dwell in your hearts through faith.

A Promise: Philippians 4:19
Fill in the blanks.

And my God will meet all your _ _ _ _ _ according to his glorious
_ _ _ _ _ _ in Christ Jesus.

And my God will meet all your **needs** according to his glorious
riches in Christ Jesus.

Questions: What are our *NEEDS*? What are our *GREEDS*?
(Define a **greed** as something we do not **need**.)

First list four *NEEDS* and then four *GREEDS.*

Four **NEEDS**

1.
2.
3.
4.

Four **GREEDS**

1.
2.
3.
4.

If in a group, ask people to share their **needs** and there is likely to
be a fairly harmonious list, but it is possible that some will put
forward things that are not really **needs**.

Also there is another point; e.g. a television is not a **basic** need; but
is it a **need** in today's society?

**Question: What else are not basic needs, but are considered
needs in today's society.**

If in a group, discuss the above question and ask people to share their **greeds** and discuss them.

So ….

Question: What are our *needs?*

Can we come to a basic list of things. Not only material items such as food, drink, clothing, shelter, warmth etc., but also emotional needs; e.g. love, friendships. What about faith?

Question: What are our *greeds?*

We suggested that a 'greed' was something that we did not 'need' but that may not be a good definition. Can we come to a well-defined list as to what our **greeds** are? Can we even define what our **greeds** are? What about the teenager who wants designer clothes and trainers? Is that a **greed**? Or are they just trying to survive in a materialistic world?

Consider the questions raised in the above paragraph and if in a group, discuss them.

The BIG Question: SO….. if God is so rich toward us …. what should our response be?

Ephesians 2:8-10
Fill in the blanks.

For it is by grace you have been saved, through faith – and this not from yourselves, it is the gift of God – not by works, so that no one can boast. For we are God's workmanship, *created in Christ Jesus*
__ __ ____ _____, which God prepared in advance for us to do.

For it is by grace that you have been saved, through faith and this not from yourselves, it is the gift of God not by works, so that no one can boast. For we are God's workmanship, *created in Christ Jesus* **to do good works**, which God prepared in advance for us to do.

Question: What should those 'good works' be?
Ephesians 4:1-3 sets the tone.

As a prisoner for the Lord, then, I urge you to live a life worthy of the calling you have received.

Question: What do we have to do to live a life worthy of our calling?

Be completely humble and gentle; be patient, bearing with one another in love.

Question: How can we do that?

By making...

... every effort to keep the unity of the Spirit through the bond of peace.

Question: What do we have to do?

Paul gives some **dos** and **don'ts** in the practical parts of his letters. We shall look at just four of them.

STOP THIS ... and ... DO THAT!

Ephesians 4:28
Fill in the blanks.

He who has been _ _ _ _ _ _ _ _ must _ _ _ _ _ no longer, but must
_ _ _ _, doing something useful with his own hands, that he may
have something to _ _ _ _ _ with those in need.

> He who has been **stealing** must **steal** no longer, but must **work**,
> doing something useful with his own hands, that he may have
> something to **share** with those in **need**.

Ephesians 6:5-8
Fill in the blanks.

Slaves, _ _ _ _ your earthly masters with respect and fear, and with
sincerity of heart, just as you would _ _ _ _ Christ. _ _ _ _ them not
only to win their favour when their eye is on you, but like slaves of
Christ, doing the will of God from your heart. Serve
wholeheartedly, as if you were serving the Lord, not men, because
you know that the Lord will _ _ _ _ _ _ _ everyone for whatever
good he does, whether he is slave or free.

> Slaves, **obey** your earthly masters with respect and fear, and
> with sincerity of heart, just as you would **obey** Christ. **Obey** not
> only to win their favour when their eye is on you, but like slaves
> of Christ, doing the will of God from your heart. Serve
> wholeheartedly, as if you were serving the Lord, not men,
> because you know that the Lord will **reward** everyone for
> whatever good he does, whether he is slave or free.

We usually apply this passage to employees and employers, and
that is a good application. So we should carry out our duties
whether or not the boss is around, but why? Not only because that
is right and proper, it is also the will of our Heavenly Father. But,
and here is more of his **riches**, He will **reward** everyone for
whatever good that person does. Therefore let us do good as Paul
puts it in Galatians 6:10:

Therefore, as we have opportunity, let us do good to all people, especially to those who belong to the family of believers.

1 Timothy 6:17-18
Fill in the blanks

Command those who are _ _ _ _ in this present world not to be arrogant nor to put their hope in wealth, which is so _ _ _ _ _ _ _ _ _, but to put their hope in God, who _ _ _ _ _ provides us with everything for our enjoyment.

Command them to do good, to be _ _ _ _ in _ _ _ _ , _ _ _ and to be _ _ _ _ _ _ _ _ and willing to _ _ _ _ _.

> Command those who are **rich** in this present world not to be arrogant nor to put their hope in **wealth**, which is so **uncertain** but to put their hope in God, who **richly** provides us with everything for our enjoyment.

> Command them to do **good** to be **rich** in **good deeds**, and to be **generous** and willing to **share**.

Question: Why were these commands given?

1 Timothy 6:19
Fill in the blanks.

In this way they will lay up _ _ _ _ _ _ _ _ for themselves as a firm foundation for the coming age, so that they may take hold of the life that is truly life.

> In this way they will lay up **treasure** for themselves as a firm foundation for the **coming** age, so that they may take hold of the life that is truly life.

The riches of this world are very uncertain as we have seen pension prospects collapse as the stock market has declined and interest rates drop. The housing market is uncertain and prices fall as interest rates rise! And job security, and so dependable income, are things of the past.

> "Do not store up for yourselves treasures on earth, where moth and rust destroy, and where thieves break in and steal. But store up for yourselves treasures in heaven, where moth and rust do not destroy, and where thieves do not break in and steal. For where your treasure is, there your heart will be also." (Matthew 6:19-21)

Paul was but echoing the sentiments of our Lord Jesus. By using the riches we have in this life for others, we will stor3 far greater riches for our eternal future.

WARNING!

1 Timothy 6:8-10
Fill in the blanks.

But if we have _ _ _ _ and _ _ _ _ _ _ _ _ _, we will be content with that. People who want to get _ _ _ _ fall into temptation and a trap and into many foolish and harmful desires that plunge men into ruin and destruction. For the _ _ _ _ of money is a root of all kinds of evil. Some people, eager for _ _ _ _ _, have wandered from the faith and pierced themselves with many griefs.

> But if we have **food** and **clothing**, we will be **content** with that. People who want to get **rich** fall into temptation and a trap and into many foolish and harmful desires that plunge men into ruin and destruction. For the **love** of money is a root of all kinds of

evil. Some people, eager for **money**, have wandered from the faith and pierced themselves with many griefs.

Christians should be good living, content people, as Paul put it a little earlier:

But godliness with contentment is great gain. (1 Timothy 6:6)

Hence being godly, but begrudging what we have to do and what we have not to do, does not make us content. We should be content when all our needs have been met. However, in an affluent, materialistic society, there is a danger, especially for the young, that they will race after money. This is a great danger for the Christian. We need enough but the desire for much more can seriously damage our faith.

We can be imitators of God

Getting the balance right
Blessings and response

**1. God is rich towards us,
we should be rich towards others**

**2. He is rich in mercy towards us,
we should be rich in mercy toward others.**

**3. He freely forgives us,
we should freely forgive others.**

**4. God gave us His Son,
what can we give others?**

Question: Which of the first three do we find the (a) easiest, (b) hardest?

Consider this question: if in a group, discuss it.

Reach out to people Help people

We should give money to the church and charities but what can we give to individuals, many of whom are not short of money and are in no need of material items? Time, compassion, sympathy, may be three things.

Question: What else can we give others?

Think about answers to this last question. If in a group, please discuss the question.

Study 3.
God in us

God's Holy Spirit is sealed inside us
Ephesians 1:13-14

And you also were included in Christ when you heard the word of truth, the gospel of your salvation. Having believed, you were marked in him with a seal, the promised Holy Spirit, who is a deposit guaranteeing our inheritance until the redemption of those who are God's possession – to the praise of his glory.

This passage makes it clear that Christians are sealed with the Holy Spirit, and Ephesians 4:30 states that the seal will not be broken until the day of redemption.

Question: What is "the gospel of salvation"?

There are a number of key words:

1. **Sin**
2. **Faith, belief** or **trust** – three English words which translate one Greek word *pistis.*
3. **Jesus Christ**
4. Christ's **death** and
5. His **resurrection**.

There are many ways the gospel of salvation can be expressed but all should include the fact that we are **sinners**, and that we **believe** that Jesus **died** for our sins, and that He **rose** from the dead.

1 Corinthians 15:3-4

1 Corinthians 15:2 mentions the gospel and then Paul goes on to explain that this is of 'first importance'.
Fill in the blanks.

For what I received I passed on to you as of first importance: that Christ _ _ _ _ for our _ _ _ _ according to the Scriptures, that he was _ _ _ _ _ _, that he was _ _ _ _ _ _ on the third day according to the Scriptures.

> For what I received I passed on to you as of first importance: that Christ **died** for our **sins** according to the Scriptures, that he was **buried**, that he was **raised** on the third day according to the Scriptures.

Question: Do you know an acronym for GOSPEL?

G - _ _ _ ' _
O - _ _ _
S - _ _ _
P - _ _ _ _ _ _ _ _
E - _ _ _ _ _ _ _
L - _ _ _ _

One acronym for **Gospel**

G - **God's**
O - **own**
S - **Son**
P - **purchased**
E - **eternal**
L - **life**

Romans 4:25

Fill in the blanks.

He [Jesus] was delivered over to _ _ _ _ _ for our _ _ _ _ and was
_ _ _ _ _ _ to life for our justification.

He [Jesus] was delivered over to **death** for our **sins** and was
raised to life for our justification.

Important

**We are sealed with God's Spirit
WHEN we believe the gospel of salvation,
that Christ died for our sins,
and was raised from the dead.**

It is important to note that although the Apostles and some of the
early Jewish Christians had to wait for the Holy Spirit during the
time covered by the Acts of the Apostles, the teaching in the letters
is that believers are sealed with God's Holy Spirit at the point of
salvation, when they believed the gospel of salvation (e.g.
Ephesians 1:13-14).

Question: What does 'guarantee' mean? (Ephesians 1:13-14)

When we buy something new there is usually a guarantee that if it
goes wrong within a year it will be repaired or even replaced. *God's
guarantee is eternal.* Ephesians 1:13-14 states because believers
are sealed with the Holy Spirit their eternal inheritance is
guaranteed. Ephesians 4:30 makes it clear that the believer is sealed
with the Holy Spirit until the day of redemption; that is the day
Christ returns and the dead are raised.

Christ can dwell in our heart by faith

Ephesians 3:16-17 is a prayer for this.
Fill in the blanks.

I pray that out of his glorious _ _ _ _ _ he [God] may _ _ _ _ _ _ _
_ _ _ you with power through his _ _ _ _ _ _ in your _ _ _ _ _ being,
so that Christ may dwell in your hearts through faith.

> I pray that our of his glorious **riches** he [God] may **strengthen**
> you with **power** through his **Spirit** in your **inner** being, so that
> Christ may dwell in your hearts through faith.

Although it is true that the Holy Spirit is sealed inside every
Christian, it is not true that Christ dwells in the heart of each and
every one. This prayer shows that for that to happen people need to
be strengthened with God's power in their inner being. Why is that?
We shall come to that in a moment.

Question: What does "dwell" mean?

This is a *homely* word. To 'dwell' somewhere, means to 'feel at
home' there. Thus for Christ to 'feel at home' in our heart, we need
to be strengthened with power in our inner being. Why?

**BIG question: Are you comfortable with the idea that Christ
could dwell inside you?**

Yes   No   Don't know   Depends

Putting this question a different way;

**Question: Are you convinced that Christ would 'be at home' in
your heart?**

This is not an easy question to answer. I suppose the honest answer would be 'sometimes'. At other times, when we get angry, for instance, we might feel very uncomfortable at the thought of Christ being inside us and being a very personal witness of what we have done. Thus we might think that the reason we need to be strengthened with power through the Spirit in our inner being before Christ can dwell in our hearts, is so that we will lead better lives, more holy lives, and there may be considerable truth in that. However, if we read Ephesians 3:17-19, we see we need power for something else.

> And I pray that you, being rooted and established in love, may have power, together with all the saints, to grasp how wide and long and high and deep is the love of Christ, and to know this love that surpasses knowledge – that you may be filled to the measure of all the fulness of God.

We may need a greater appreciation of God's love for us before Christ can feel at home in our heart. We need to appreciate that God loves us in spite of our sin, and Christ can dwell in us in spite of our sin.

Paul said the following

Galatians 2:20.
Fill in the blanks.

I have been crucified with Christ and I no longer live, but _ _ _ _ _ _ lives in me. The life I live in the body, I live by faith in the Son of God, who loved me and gave himself for me.

> I have been crucified with Christ and I no longer live, but **Christ** lives in me. The life I live in the body, I live by faith in the Son of God, who loved me and gave himself for me.

Can we say the same as Paul?

Yes   No   Don't know   Not yet

If in a group, ask people to share their answers, but be encouraging. Some may feel they will never get to the position where Christ could 'feel at home' in their hearts. Others may feel they are not quite ready; the time may be 'not yet'. They may need to learn the depth of God's love for them.

God dwells in a temple.

Question: Which temple is this?

The only buildings that God was said to dwell in were (a) the tabernacle, the tent in the wilderness, and (b) the temple in Jerusalem.

Question: "Who" is the temple?

Paul makes it clear that God, through His Holy Spirit, no longer dwells in a physical building, but inside all believers. Collectively, in this dispensation, all Christians make up God's temple.

Ephesians 2:19-22.
Fill in the blanks.

You are no longer _ _ _ _ _ _ _ _ _ _ and _ _ _ _ _ _, but
_ _ _ _ _ _ _ _ _ _ _ _ _ with _ _ _' _ people and _ _ _ _ _ _ _
of _ _ _' _ household, built on the _ _ _ _ _ _ _ _ _ _ of the apostles
and prophets, with Christ Jesus himself as the chief
_ _ _ _ _ _ _ _ _ _ _. In him the whole _ _ _ _ _ _ _ _ is joined
together and rises to become a holy _ _ _ _ _ _ in the Lord. And in
him _ _ _ too are being _ _ _ _ _ together to become a

_ _ _ _ _ _ _ _ in which _ _ _ lives by his Spirit.

Consequently, you are no longer **foreigners** and **aliens**, but **fellow citizens** with **God's** people and **members** of **God's** household, built on the **foundation** of the apostles and prophets, with Christ Jesus himself as the chief **cornerstone.** In him the whole **building** is joined together and rises to become a holy **temple** in the Lord. And in him **you** too are being **built** together to become a **dwelling** in which **God** lives by his Spirit.

This is an incredible passage in its historical setting. The Gentiles were, at one time, foreigners and aliens (Ephesians 1:11-12). However, when they believed in Christ, they became fellow citizens with God's people and members of God's household, and that is still the situation today. When someone becomes a Christian they become fellow citizens with us, and fellow members of God's household. This house is built upon Jesus Christ; He is the foundation; He is the chief corner stone. However, the bricks of this building are us, Christians. We are being built together to make a holy temple, to make a dwelling, in which God lives by His Spirit. Remember, as soon as a person believes the gospel of salvation, they are sealed with the Spirit; they become a brick in this building.

Revelation 3:12.
Fill in the blanks.

Him who overcomes I will make a _ _ _ _ _ _ in the _ _ _ _ _ _ of my God. Never again will he leave it. I will write on him the _ _ _ _ of my God and the _ _ _ _ of the city of my God, the new Jerusalem, which is coming down out of heaven from my God; and I will also write on him my new _ _ _ _.

"Him who overcomes I [Jesus] will make a **pillar** in the **temple** of my God. Never again will he leave it. I will write on him the **name** of my God and the **name** of the city of my God, the new Jerusalem, which is coming down out of heaven from my God; and I will also write on him my new **name**"

Question: What do you think Christ's new name will be when He comes again?

If with a group, see if people have any suggestions and discuss them. Some have suggested that Christ's new name will be 'Jehovah', but that is not a *new* name. I don't think we know what that new name will be.

Question: What do you think is the significance of writing God's name on a person?

Again, if with a group discuss the various answers. One aspect of writing God's name on a person is 'ownership'. We have been redeemed. Christ died for our sins and we have been 'bought back' from the slave market of sin and death. Thus we are His. We belong to Him and His name is written on us.

BIG Question: SO ... what should our response be?

Ephesians 2:8-10.
Fill in the blanks.

For it by grace you have been saved, through faith - and this not from yourselves, it is the gift of God - not by works, so that no one can boast. For we are God's workmanship, *created in Christ Jesus*
__ __ ____ _____, which God prepared in advance for us to do.

For it by grace you have been saved, through faith - and this not from yourselves, it is the gift of God - not by works, so that no one can boast. For we are God's workmanship, *created in Christ Jesus* **to do good works**, which God prepared in advance for us to do.

Question: So ... what should those good works be?

Let's read first Ephesians 4:1-3

As a prisoner for the Lord, then I urge you to live a life worthy of the calling you have received.

Question: What do we have to do to live a life worthy of our calling?

Be completely humble and gentle;
be patient, bearing with one another in love.

Question: How can we be like that?

Make every effort to keep the unity of the Spirit through the bond of peace.

Question: What do we have to do?

Paul gives some good advice later on in Ephesians.

1. **Do not grieve the Holy Spirit of God with whom you were sealed for the day of redemption.**

Question: What do we do that grieves the Holy Spirit?

Question: How can we stop grieving Him?

Paul tells us both the negative and the positive.

Ephesians 4:28-32
Fill in the blanks

He who has been _ _ _ _ _ _ _ _ must _ _ _ _ _ no longer, but must work, doing something useful with his own hands, that he may have something to _ _ _ _ _ with those in need. Do not let any _ _ _ _ _ _ _ _ _ _ _ talk come out of your mouths, but only what is _ _ _ _ _ _ _ for building others up according to their needs, that it may _ _ _ _ _ _ _ those who listen.

And do not grieve the Holy Spirit of God, with whom you were sealed for the day of redemption.

Get rid of all _ _ _ _ _ _ _ _ _ _ _, _ _ _ _ and _ _ _ _ _ _, _ _ _ _ _ _ _ _ and _ _ _ _ _ _ _, along with every form of _ _ _ _ _ _. Be _ _ _ _ and _ _ _ _ _ _ _ _ _ _ _ _ _ _ to one another. _ _ _ _ _ _ _ _ _ each other, just as in Christ God forgave you.

What do we do that grieves the Holy Spirit? How can we stop grieving Him? Ephesians 4:28-32 tells us both the negative and the positive.

He who has been **stealing** must **steal** no longer, but must work, doing something useful with his own hands, that he may have something to **share** with those in need. Do not let any **unwholesome** talk come out of your mouths, but only what is **helpful** for building others up according to their needs, that it may **benefit** those who listen.

And do not grieve the Holy Spirit of God, with whom you were sealed for the day of redemption.

Get rid of all **bitterness**, **rage** and **anger**, **brawling** and **slander**, along with every form of **malice**. Be **kind** and **compassionate** to one another, **forgiving** each other, just as in Christ God forgave you.

The negatives that grieve the Holy Spirit include stealing, unwholesome talk, bitterness, rage, anger, brawling, slander and malice. The positives which please the Holy Spirit include sharing, helping, benefiting, kindness, compassion and forgiving.

Question: Which of the negatives do you have difficulty controlling?

Question: Which of the positives do you have difficulty doing?

Note: If doing this with a group, please ask them to discuss these last two questions.

2. Do not grieve the Holy Spirit of God

Question: What do we do that grieves the Holy Spirit?

Question: How can we stop grieving Him?

Answer: By being filled with the Spirit!

Ephesians 5:18-19 again, gives us some negatives and positives.
Fill in the blanks

Do not get _ _ _ _ _ on _ _ _ _, which leads to debauchery.
Instead, be filled with the Spirit. Speak to one another with
_ _ _ _ _ _, _ _ _ _ _ and spiritual songs. _ _ _ _ and make

_ _ _ _ _ in your heart to the Lord, always giving _ _ _ _ _ _ to God the Father for everything, in the name of our Lord Jesus Christ.

> Do not get **drunk** on **wine**, which leads to debauchery. Instead, be filled with the Spirit. Speak to one another with **psalms, hymns** and **spiritual** songs. **Sing** and make **music** in your heart to the Lord, always giving **thanks** to God the Father for everything, in the name of our Lord Jesus Christ.

Drunkenness will grieve the Holy Spirit. Instead we should be filled with the Spirit and this will result in an attitude of praise and thankfulness.

Question: Which of the following *grieves* the Holy Spirit and which *pleases* Him?

		Grieves	Pleases
1	stealing		
2	working		
3	sharing		
4	bad talk		
5	being helpful		
6	benefiting		
7	bitterness		
8	rage		
9	anger		
10	brawling		
11	slander		
12	malice		
13	kindness		

14	compassion		
15	forgiving		
16	drunkenness		
17	debauchery		
18	singing psalms		
19	singing hymns		
20	thankfulness		

The answers should be fairly obvious. Numbers 1 to 12 grieves the Holy Spirit; 13 to 20 pleases Him.

Task: List three *other* things which grieve the Spirit and three *others* which please Him.

Grieves	Pleases

Note: If in a group, have a discussion about the different answers people give. Deal with what grieves the Holy Spirit first and afterwards what pleases Him. Be positive and concentrate on what *pleases* Him. Remember what *grieves* Him are sins, and these have been forgiven and God no longer remembers them..

3. Find out what pleases the Lord

Ephesians 5:8-10 contains this instruction.
Fill in the blanks

For you were once _____, but now you are _____ in the Lord. Live as children of _____ (for the fruit of the _____ consists in all _____, _____ and _____) and find out what **pleases** the Lord.

> For you were once **darkness**, but now you are **light** in the Lord. Live as children of **light** (for the fruit of the **light** consists in all **goodness**, **righteousness** and **truth**) and find out what pleases the Lord.

Question: Where can we find out "what *pleases* the Lord"?

Note: If in a group, compare and discuss the answers.

Here are some possible answers.

    (a) The Bible should rank high in the list of answers.
    (b) The 'good works' that we have been covering in these studies is another.
    (c) Read Philippians 4:8-9 for other things.

This question has been dealing with 'where' we can find out what pleases the Lord. It does not ask 'what' pleases the Lord.

Question: What pleases the Lord?

Note: If in a group, compare and discuss the answers.

Here are some possible answers.

    (a) The fruit of the Spirit is a good answer (Galatians 5:22-23).
    (b) The fruit of the light, in this passage, which is goodness, righteousness and truth.
    (c) The fruit of righteousness (Philippians 1:11).

(d) Loving God with all our heart, our soul and our might; loving fellow Christians as Christ loves them and gave Himself for them; loving neighbours as ourselves.

(e) Read Colossians 3:1-2.

4. We are the Temple of God

Do not pollute the temple! Do not pollute God's dwelling place. This will surely grieve God's Holy Spirit.

Question: How can we pollute the temple of God? That is, how can we pollute ourselves?

Note: If in a group, compare and discuss the various answers.

One answer may be 'sin', but we are all sinners and come short of the glory of God. To *pollute* may require some serious sins.

We have a good example in 1 Corinthians 6:15-20.
Fill in the blanks.

Do you not know that your bodies are members of Christ himself? Shall I then take the members of Christ and unite them with a _ _ _ _ _ _ _ _ _ _ ? Never!
Do you not know that he who unites himself with a _ _ _ _ _ _ _ _ _ _ is one with her in _ _ _ _ ? For it is said, "The two will become one flesh". But he who unites himself with the Lord is one with him in spirit.
Flee from _ _ _ _ _ _ immorality. All other sins a man commits are outside his _ _ _ _ , but he who sins sexually sins against his own _ _ _ _ .
Do you not know that your body is a temple of the Holy Spirit who is in you, whom you have received from God? You are not your own; you were bought at a price.

Therefore _ _ _ _ _ _ God with your _ _ _ _.

Do you not know that your bodies are members of Christ himself? Shall I then take the members of Christ and unite them with a **prostitute**? Never!

Do you not know that he who unites himself with a **prostitute** is one with her in **body**? For it is said, "The two will become one flesh." But he who unites himself with the Lord is one with him in spirit.

Flee from **Sexual** immorality. All other sins a man commits are outside his **body**, but he who sins sexually sins against his own body.

Do you not know that your body is a temple of the Holy Spirit, who is in you, whom you have received from God? You are not your own; you were bought at a price.

Therefore **honour** God with your **body**.

Sexual intercourse with a prostitute is one way to pollute our bodies.

Question: What other ways are there?

Ephesians 5:3-4.
Fill in the blanks.

But among you there must not even be a hint of _ _ _ _ _ _ _ immorality, or of any kind of _ _ _ _ _ _ _ _, or of greed …

Question: Why not?

… because these are _ _ _ _ _ _ _ _ for God's holy people. Nor should there be _ _ _ _ _ _ _ _ _, foolish talk or _ _ _ _ _ _ joking, which are out of place, but rather _ _ _ _ _ _ _ _ _ _ _ _.

But among you there must not be even a hint of **sexual** immorality, or of any kind of **impurity**, or of greed, because these are **improper** for God's holy people. Nor should there be **obscenity**, foolish talk or **coarse** joking, which are out of place, but rather **thanksgiving**.

It would seem that if God dwells within us, not only is it wrong and inconsistent to have sexual intercourse with a prostitute, all sexual immorality is wrong. That is any sex outside of marriage.

But not only is the sex act immoral, so, too, can be the things we say; the obscenities and coarse joking. These are simply out of place for the Christian, and they will grieve the Holy Spirit.

Question: But why is the Bible so against sex outside of marriage?

The Bible says that "all other sins a man commits are outside his body, he who sins sexually sins against his own body."

Question: In what ways are sexual sins, sins against our bodies?

Task: List some of the problems sexual sins cause.

Here are some examples of 'sins against our bodies':
   (a) sexually transmitted diseases;
   (b) AIDS;
   (c) unwanted pregnancies.

Other problems are
   (d) broken marriages, and generally weakening the family;
   (e) single mothers and the difficulties they and their children have.

Sexual permissiveness was rife in the Roman Empire, as were sexually transmitted diseases. When writing to the Romans Paul stated:

> Because of this, God gave them over to shameful lusts. Even their women exchanged natural relations for unnatural ones.
>
> In the same way the men also abandoned natural relations with women and were inflamed with lust for one another. Men committed indecent acts with other men, and received in themselves the due penalty for their perversion. (Romans 1:26-17)

The 'due penalty for their perversion' was probably the sexually transmitted diseases.

Question: Are there any other activities which are "sins against our own body"?

Note: If in a group, compare, contrast and discuss the different answers.

If we take this expression "sins against our own body" to mean those things that will harm our bodies, then we may want to include:

(a) smoking, although that is often not seen as a sin;
(b) excessive alcohol, which can damage the liver;
(c) drugs;
(d) gluttony, which can cause obesity and diabetes.

Question: What others are there?

Pornography, obscenity, coarse joking can detrimentally affect the mind; see Ephesians 5:3-4.

Getting the balance right

Blessings and response

God dwells in us.

We should ensure our bodies are pure and clean:
a fit place for Him to live.

Study 4.
Love

Ephesians 1:4-6

For he [God] chose us in him [Christ] before the creation of the world to be holy and blameless in his sight. In **love** he predestined us to be adopted as his sons through Jesus Christ, in accordance with his pleasure and will - to the praise of his glorious grace, which he has freely given us in the One he loves.

Question: What is love?

The best definition is found in 1 Corinthians 13:4-8.
Fill in the blanks.

Love is _ _ _ _ _ _ _ ,

      love is _ _ _ _ ,

Love does not _ _ _ _ ,

      It does not _ _ _ _ _ ,

         It is not _ _ _ _ _ ,

Love is not _ _ _ _ ,

      It is not _ _ _ _ - _ _ _ _ _ _ _ ,

         It is not easily _ _ _ _ _ _ _ ,

           It keeps no record of _ _ _ _ _ _ _ .

Love does not delight in _ _ _ _

    but rejoices with the _ _ _ _ _.

Love always _ _ _ _ _ _ _ _,

    always _ _ _ _ _ _,

       always _ _ _ _ _,

         always _ _ _ _ _ _ _ _ _ _.

Love never _ _ _ _ _.

1 Corinthians 13:4-8 defines love as a love of *actions*, not a love of *feelings*.

The positives: Love is ...

- Love is **patient**,
- love is **kind**.

The negatives: Love is not ...

- It does not **envy**,
- it does not **boast**,
- it is not **proud**.
- It is not **rude**,
- it is not **self-seeking**,
- it is not easily **angered**,
- it keeps no record of **wrongs**.
- Love does not delight in **evil** but

More positives: Love ...

- Love ... rejoices with the **truth**.

- It always **protects**,
- always **trusts**,
- always **hopes**,
- always **perseveres**.
- Love never **fails**.

Note: The Greek word for love is *agape.*

> *Agape* is unconquerable benevolence, undefeatable good-will; it is the spirit which will never seek anything but the other person's good, no matter what the other person does ...This Christian love is undefeatable caring. (William Barclay)

Such is God's love for us. It is a high and holy love. So high and holy, the word *agape* hardly ever occurs in secular Greek writings.

Question? Will God's love ever fail us?

Yes   No   Don't know

Answer: No!

We have just read, "Love never fails".

Question: But what if we do something very bad?

WE may grieve God but remember *agape love* "is the spirit which will never seek anything but the other person's good, no matter what the other person does". And we can see His great love for people like David in the Old Testament and Paul in the New; two people who did terrible things. Paul knew this and wrote:

> Who shall separate us from the love of Christ? Shall trouble or hardship or persecution or famine or nakedness or danger or

sword? As it is written: "For your sake we face death all day long; we are considered as sheep to be slaughtered." No, in all these things we are more than conquerors through him who loved us. For I am convinced that neither death nor life, neither angels nor demons, neither the present nor the future, nor any powers, neither height nor depth, nor anything else in all creation, will be able to separate us from the love of God that is in Christ Jesus our Lord. (Romans 8:35-39)

Christians need to be reassured and convinced, that their heavenly Father will never stop loving.

Question: What it would take for you to stop loving your children?

Note: If in a group, compare and discuss answers.

Note: The answer is often … "Nothing1 I will always love them!" If we sinners can love like that, then what about the love of our Heavenly Father who is sinless.

A Prayer for understanding love

Paul knew that Christians would have problems trying to understand just how vast God's love is; hence the prayer in Ephesians 3:17-19.

Fill in the blanks.

And I pray that you, being rooted and established in _ _ _ _, may have _ _ _ _ _, together with all the saints, to grasp how _ _ _ _ and _ _ _ _ and _ _ _ _ and _ _ _ _ is the _ _ _ _ of Christ, and to [get to] know this _ _ _ _ that surpasses knowledge - [so] that you may be filled to the measure of all the _ _ _ _ _ _ _ _ of God.

And I pray that you, being rooted and established in **love**, may have **power**, together with all the saints, to grasp how **wide** and **long** and **high** and **deep** is the **love** of Christ, and to know this **love** that surpasses knowledge - [so] that you may be filled to the measure of all the **fullness** of God.

Question: Will we ever fully comprehend God's love?

Probably not, but as we progress through life and grow in our faith, we should have more and more understanding of God's love, and have more assurance of it never failing.

Question: How will we be able to [get to] know something which surpasses knowledge?

"Rooted and established (grounded)" is a gardening term. We are loved by God but to begin to understand that love, we need to be "rooted and established" in love ourselves. That is we need to be loved and to love, however inadequate that love may be.

Then, having been "rooted and established", we need God's enabling power for us to grasp just how extensive His love is; that He loves not only super Christians like Peter and Paul, He also loves you and me. But not only you and me, He loves the world (John 3:16). This is what Paul wrote:

Ephesians 2:4-5.
Fill in the blanks.

But because of his _ _ _ _ _ _ _ _ _ for us, God, who is _ _ _ _ in _ _ _ _ _, made us _ _ _ _ _ with Christ even when we were _ _ _ _ in transgressions - it is by _ _ _ _ _ you have been

_ _ _ _ _.

But because of his **great love** for us, God who is **rich** in **mercy**, made us **alive** with Christ even when we were **dead** in transgressions - it is by **grace** you have been **saved**.

Question: What does it mean to be saved?

Question: What are we saved *from*?

What are we saved *for*?

If in a group: discuss the answers to these questions. Important points are:

- We are saved *from* the consequences of sin and death.
- We are saved (a) *for* good works in this life and (b) *for* eternal life, when God will show us the unsearchable riches of His grace.

Big question: So what should our response be to the fact that God loves us, and will never fail to love us, and nothing can separate us from His love?

Ephesians 2:8-10 gives us the general orders.
Fill in the blanks.

For it is by grace you have been saved, through faith - and this is not from yourselves, it is the gift of God - not by works, so that no one can boast. For we are God's workmanship, *created in Christ Jesus* _ _ _ _ _ _ _ _ _ _ _ _ _ _, which God prepared in advance for us to do.

For it is by grace you have been saved, through faith - and this not from yourselves, it is the gift of God - not by works, so that no one can boast. For we are God's workmanship, created in

Christ Jesus **to do good works**, which God prepared in advance for us to do.

So what should those 'good works' be?
Ephesians 4:1-3 sets the tone.

> As a prisoner for the Lord, then, I urge you to live a life worthy of the calling you have received.

Question: What do we have to do to live a life worthy of our calling?

> Be completely humble and gentle; be patient, bearing with one another in love.

Question: How can we do that?

By making...

> ... every effort to keep the unity of the Spirit through the bond of peace.

Question: What do we have to do?

Ephesians says quite a lot about what our response should be. One of the things is that we should believe, have faith and trust in what God has said.

1. We could be (should be?) like the Ephesians.

They had "faith" in the Lord, and "love" for fellow-Christians.

Ephesians 1:15-16.
Fill in the blanks.

For this reason, ever since I [Paul] heard about your _ _ _ _ _ in the Lord Jesus and your _ _ _ _ for all the saints, I have not stopped giving _ _ _ _ _ _ for you, remembering you in my _ _ _ _ _ _ _.

For this reason, ever since I heard about your **faith** in the Lord Jesus and your **love** for all the saints, I have not stopped giving **thanks** for you, remembering you in my **prayers**.

Question? What is faith? What is your definition?
Note: If in a group, discuss the different answers.

Hebrews 11:1 gives a good definition, and so does Romans 4:20-21.

Now **faith** is **being sure** of what we hope for and **certain** of what we do not see. (Hebrews 11:1)

Yet he (Abraham) did not waver through unbelief regarding the promise of God, but was **strengthened in his faith** and gave glory to God, being **fully persuaded that God had power to do what he had promised**. (Romans 4:20-21)

- In Hebrews faith in "being sure" and "being certain".
- In Romans faith is being "fully persuaded" that God has the power to do what He says He will.

Can you think of an acronym for FAITH?

        F -   _ _ _ _ _ _ _ _ _

        A -   _ _ _

        I -   _

        T -   _ _ _ _ _

        H -   _ _ _

An acronym for FAITH.

F	-	**Forsaking**
A	-	**All**
I	-	**I**
T	-	**Trust**
H	-	**Him**

Question: Were the Ephesians perfect in their love?
Note: Please explain why or why not with examples.

Answer: No!

They were not. If we read through the latter part of Ephesians, starting at 4:17 onwards, we will see them being told to stop a number of things that were incompatible with love.

For example, they were told to stop falsehood and start to speak the truth; to stop stealing and start working; to get rid of all bitterness, rage, anger, brawling, slander and malice, and instead be kind, compassionate and forgiving to one another (Ephesians 4:25, 28, 31-32).

We might think all this terrible, but we must remember that many of the Gentile Christians had lived a pagan society, with immoral backgrounds. They had started on the Christian pathway and were learning love, and Paul praised them for it and thanked God for it.

2. We should bear with one another in love.

Question: What does it mean to "bear" with one another in love?

Answer: Read Ephesians 4:1-3.

To give us a better understanding, here are some different translations of Ephesians 4:2.

> With all lowliness and meekness, with longsuffering, forbearing one another in love. (*KJV*)

> Living as becomes you - with complete lowliness of mind (humility) and meekness (unselfishness, gentleness, mildness), with patience, bearing with one another and making allowances because you love one another. (*Amplified*)

> Be humble and gentle. Be patient with each other, making allowances for each other's faults because of your love. (*Living Bible*)

> Be humble always and gentle, and patient too. Be forbearing with one another and charitable. *(New English Bible)*

Note: This shows the benefits of reading more than one translation of the Bible.

3. We should speak the truth in love

Note Ephesians 4:15

> Instead, speaking the truth in love, we will in all things grow up into him who is the Head, that is Christ.

Question: What does it mean to "speak the truth"?

Note: If in a group, compare and discuss different answers.

Question: what does it mean to speak the truth "IN LOVE"?

Note: Again, if in a group, compare and discuss answers.

The general principle may be best summed up in the words of an old song; "It ain't what you say, it's the way that you say it!"

> Let your conversation be always full of grace, seasoned with salt, so that you may know how to answer everyone. (Colossians 4:6)

Like the old song, this is concerned not so much with "what" we answer, but with "how" we answer.

4. We should be "imitators of God".

Read Ephesians 5:1-2.

Be imitators of God, therefore, as dearly loved children and live a life of love, just as Christ loved us and gave himself up for us as a fragrant offering and sacrifice to God.

Question: What must we do to be "imitators" of God?

Note: If in a group, compare and discuss the answers.

Ephesians 5:1-2 highlights to aspects.

> (a) live a life of love
> (b) be like Christ, and give up things for others.

Question: Who else should we imitate?

Note: If in a group, compare and discuss the answers.

The Christian will naturally want to imitate Christ. "What would Jesus do?" has been a very popular slogan and this, perhaps, should be our ideal. But for new Christians the thought of imitating Christ is awesome, overwhelming. It was the same in the New Testament times and it is interesting that Paul wrote the following to the Philippians.

> Join with others in following my example, brothers, and take note of those who live according to the pattern we gave you. (Philippians 3:17)

So for these Christians he was telling them to imitate himself and others who lived according to the Christian pattern.

> Follow my example, as I follow the example of Christ. (1 Corinthians 11:1)

So it is essential for older and mature Christians to be imitators of God and follow Christ in the way they live. In doing this they set the example for younger and less mature Christians. For the latter, it is easier to follow Christians, whom they can see, than Christ, whom they cannot.

5. Husbands should love our wives! But how?

Note Ephesians 5:25-33: Husbands, love your wives!

Question: How should husbands love their wives?

Note: If in a group, compare and discuss the answers.

Here are three answers.

Answer 1. Ephesians 5:25-27.

Fill in the blanks.

Just as Christ _ _ _ _ _ **the church and** _ _ _ _ _ _ _ _ _ _ _ **up for her** to make her holy, cleansing her by the washing with water through the word, and to present her to himself as a radiant church, without stain or wrinkle or any other blemish, but holy and blameless.

> Husbands, love your wives, just as Christ **loved** the church and **gave himself** up for her to make her holy, cleansing her by the washing with water through the word, and to present her to himself as a radiant church, without stain or wrinkle or any other blemish, but holy and blameless.

Answer 2. Ephesians 5:28-32
Fill in the blanks.

In this same way, **husbands ought to love their wives as their own** _ _ _ _ _ _. He who loves his wife loves himself. After all, no one ever _ _ _ _ _ his own body, but he _ _ _ _ _ and _ _ _ _ _ for it, just as Christ does the church - for we are members of his body. "For this reason a man will leave his father and mother and be united to his wife, and the two will become one flesh." This is a profound mystery - but I am talking about Christ and the church.

> In this same way, husbands ought to love their wives as their own **bodies**. He who loves his wife loves himself. After all, no one ever **hated** his own body, but he **feeds** and **cares** for it, just as Christ does the church - for we are members of his body. "For this reason a man will leave his father and mother and be united to his wife, and the two will become one flesh." This is a profound mystery - but I am talking about Christ and the church.

Answer 3. Ephesians 5:33
Fill in the blanks.

However, each one of you also must **love his wife _ _   _ _
_ _ _ _ _ himself**, and the wife must respect her husband.

> However, each one of you also must love his wife **as he loves**
> himself. So whatever he does for himself, and the wife must
> respect her husband.

Here the husband should have no less love for his wife than he does
for himself. So whatever he does for himself, he should do for her.

Question: Can we love our wives like this?

Yes   No   Don't know

With God's help we can. We need, first and foremost, to put our
wives' needs above our own. This was very common in the past
when many men went without food so that their wives and children
would have sufficient to eat. Is that spirit alive today?

Note: Much of this has to do with the man being the *head* of the
woman. Some see this as authoritarian, but in the New Testament
society the head was seen as that part of the body which supplied
the needs of the body. Food and drink were taken in through the
head, so was air. We saw, heard, tasted and smelt through the head.
Thus the head provided all that the body needed. So the man, as
head of the wife, should supply all that she needed.

Note: Christ is the head of the church which is His body, and he
supplies all its needs.

And my God will meet ask your needs according to his glorious riches in Christ Jesus. (Philippians 4:19)

6. Wives should love their husban33ds

The older women were told to 'train' the younger women to love their husbands.

> Then they can train the younger women to love their husbands and children, to be self-controlled and pure, to be busy as home, to be kind, and to be subject to their husbands, so that no one will malign the word of God. (Titus 2:4-5)

Again, here, we see it is a love of actions, but we may wonder why these younger women needed training to love their husbands. Remember that at that time many were new converts from paganism and would have little idea what love and commitment meant.

7. We should love our Lord Jesus with an undying love!

Note Ephesians 6:22-24.
Fill in the blanks.

I [Paul] am sending him (Tychicus) to you for this very purpose, that you may know how we are, and that he may _ _ _ _ _ _ _ _ _ you. _ _ _ _ _ to the brothers, and _ _ _ _ with _ _ _ _ _ from God the Father and the Lord Jesus Christ. _ _ _ _ _ to all who _ _ _ _ our Lord Jesus Christ with an _ _ _ _ _ _ _ love.

> I am sending him [Tychicus] to you for this very purpose, that you may know how we are, and that he may **encourage** you. **Peace** to the brothers, and **love** with **faith** from God the Father

and the Lord Jesus Christ. **Grace** to all who **love** our Lord Jesus Christ with an **undying** love.

What a lovely ending to a letter.

Question: What do we mean by an "undying" love?

Note: If in a group, compare and discuss answers.

Some may take the line that our love should never shrink, grow smaller. Others may take the line that it should never end, we should never stop loving Him. Here are some other translations.

Grace be with all them that love our Lord Jesus Christ in sincerity. Amen. (*KJV*)

Grace (God's undeserved favour) be with all who love our Lord Jesus Christ with undying and incorruptible love. Amen - so let it be. (*Amplified*)

May God's grace and blessing be upon all who sincerely love our Lord Jesus Christ. (*Living Bible*)

God's grace be with all who love our Lord Jesus Christ with love imperishable. (*New English Bible*; margin)

We should love our Lord Jesus with an undying, never failing love, even if that love is deficient in other respects. We know that nothing can separate us from His love for us (Romans 8:35-39), so let us never stop returning the love we can give Him – even though it is a poorer love.

Note: As the *agape* love of the Bible is a love of action, and actions take time, is it possible for us to love and care for everyone? (Discuss)

Task!

We have just asked:

> As the *agape* love of the Bible is a love of action, and actions take time, is it possible for us to love and care for everyone?

Even if we have the inclination to love everyone, do we have the time to do it, let alone the energy? We shall investigate. Consider the following table:

THE TOP TEN

Person	Number
The Lord	
Parents	
Children	
Brothers/ Sisters	
Christians	
Neighbours	
Enemies	

First: Write in three other individuals / groups Christians should love. This will make the number of groups up to 10.

Note: If in a group, ask people their answers which can then be compared and discussed.

Second: Put the number 1 against the person(s) you think you should love first or most; then put a the number 2 against the second and then the number 3 against the third..

Note: If in a group, ask people their answers which can then be compared and discussed.

Third: Then put the number 4 against the person(s) you think should love fourth, and so on up to number 10.

Note: If in a group, ask people their answers which can then be compared and discussed.

Compare

Note: If in a group, when people have completed the table, discuss and compare results. There is no absolute answer. Clearly unmarried people will have different answers from those married with children. The point of the exercise is to get people to prioritise.

For me loving the Lord, my wife and my children come top of the list but enemies are at number 10. I am afraid I struggle with that one as I don't seem to have much time, energy and effort left for them!

Question: We should love others! It is a simple as that to say … but is it so simple to do?

Getting the balance right

Blessings and response

God loves us.
We should love Him.

God loves others.
We should love them also.

Study 5.
But

"But" is a great word for giving us balance.

Compare "**what we *were* in ourselves**" with "**what we *now are* in Christ**".

Read Ephesians 2:1-7
Fill in the blanks.

As for you, you **were** dead in your _ _ _ _ _ _ _ _ _ _ _ _ _ and
_ _ _ _, in which you **used** to live when you followed the _ _ _ _
of this _ _ _ _ _ and of the ruler of the kingdom of the air, the spirit
who is now at work in those who are _ _ _ _ _ _ _ _ _ _ _. All of
us also **lived** among them at one time, gratifying the
_ _ _ _ _ _ _ _ of our sinful nature and following its _ _ _ _ _ _ _
and _ _ _ _ _ _ _ _. Like the rest, we **were** by nature objects of
_ _ _ _ _.

But ...

because of His _ _ _ _ _ _ _ _ _ for us, God, who is _ _ _ _ in
_ _ _ _ _, **made us alive** with Christ even when we were _ _ _ _ in
transgressions - it is by grace you **have been saved.** And God
raised us up with Christ and **seated us** with Him in the heavenly
realms in Christ Jesus, in order that in the coming ages He **might
show** the _ _ _ _ _ _ _ _ _ _ _ _ _ _ _ _ _ _ _ of His grace, expressed
in his _ _ _ _ _ _ _ _ to us in Christ Jesus.

As for you, you **were** dead in your **transgressions** and **sins**, in which you **used** to live when you followed the **ways** of this **world** and of the ruler of the kingdom of the air, the spirit who is now at work in those who are disobedient. All of us also **lived** among them at one time, gratifying the **cravings** of our sinful nature and following its **desires** and **thoughts**. Like the rest, we were by nature *obje*cts of **wrath**.

Note: Notice the past tenses in the verses above. However, things have changed, and the 'but' at the beginning of the next verse compares and contrasts *what we are now* with what we were.

But ... because of his **great love** for us, God who is **rich** in **mercy, MADE US ALIVE** with Christ even when we were **dead** in transgressions - it is by grace you **HAVE BEEN SAVED**. And God **RAISED US UP** with Christ and **SEATED US** with Him in the heavenly realms in Christ Jesus, in order that in the coming ages He **MIGHT SHOW** the **incomparable riches** of His grace, expressed in His **kindness** to us in Christ Jesus.

What a contrast between what we were and what we are!

Note: Read Titus 3:3-5 and notice the **"BUT"**

At one time we too were foolish, disobedient, deceived and enslaved by all kinds of passions and pleasures. We lived in malice and envy, being hated and hating one another.

But ...

when the kindness and love of God our Saviour appeared, he saved us, not because of righteous things we had done, but because of his mercy. He saved us through the washing of rebirth and renewal by the Holy Spirit.

Note: Notice again what comes before the 'but' and what comes after. Compare and contrast.

Two Separations from God!

As Gentile sinners there were two things that separated us from God. The first is generally well appreciated in Christian circles, but the second is not.

1. Sin separated us from God, but we have been forgiven by believing Christ died for our sins. We have been made alive.

This was dealt with in Ephesians 2:1-7, which we have just considered.

Note: Read Colossians 1:21-22 and notice the "BUT NOW"

Once you were alienated from God and were enemies in your minds because of your evil behavior.

But now …

he has reconciled you by Christ's physical body through death to present you holy in his sight, without blemish and free from accusation.

This passage also contrasts the separation sin caused and how we have been reconciled to God by Christ's death on the cross.

2. Gentiles were separated from God, but were brought near by God abolishing the Law of Moses.

A Gentile is anyone who is *not a Jew*. The Jews were God's chosen people and they were given the Law of Moses which made them a unique nation. However, all of that changed at the end of the Acts period. Ephesians 2:11-18 explains how things changed for the Gentiles.

Read Ephesians 2:11-18
Fill in the blanks.

Therefore, *remember that formerly* you who are _ _ _ _ _ _ _ _ by birth and called "uncircumcised" by those who call themselves "the circumcision" (that done in the body by the hands of men) – remember that *at that time you were* _ _ _ _ _ _ _ _ from Christ, _ _ _ _ _ _ _ _ from citizenship in Israel and _ _ _ _ _ _ _ _ _ to the covenants of the promise, without _ _ _ _ and without _ _ _ in the world.

> Therefore, *remember that formerly* you who are **Gentiles** by birth and called "uncircumcised" by those who call themselves "the circumcision" (that done in the body by the hands of men) – remember that *at that time you were* **separate** from Christ, **excluded** from citizenship in Israel and **foreigners** to the covenants of the promise, without **hope** and without **God** in the world.

But now …

In Christ Jesus you who once *were far away* have been *brought near* through the _ _ _ _ _ of Christ. For he himself is our peace, who has *made the two one* and has destroyed the barrier, the _ _ _ _ _ _ _ _ _ _ _ _ _ of hostility, by abolishing in his flesh the _ _ _ with its _ _ _ _ _ _ _ _ _ _ _ _ _ and _ _ _ _ _ _ _ _ _ _ _ _. His purpose was *to create* in himself _ _ _ _ _ _ _ _ _ out of the two, thus **making peace**, and in this one body to *reconcile* both of them to God through the cross, by which he _ _ _ _ _ _ _ _ _ _ their hostility. He came and preached _ _ _ _ _ to you who *were far away* and _ _ _ _ _ to those who were near. For through him *we both have access* to the Father by one Spirit.

> **But now ...** in Christ Jesus you who once *were far away* have been *brought near* through the **blood** of Christ. For he himself is our peace, who has *made the two one* and has *destroyed the barrier*, the **dividing wall** of hostility, by abolishing in his flesh the law with its **commandments** and **regulations**. His purpose was *to create* in himself **one new man** out of the two, thus *making peace,* and in this one body to *reconcile* both of them to God through the cross, by which he **put to death** their hostility. He came and preached **peace** to you who *were far away* and **peace** to those who were near. For through him *we both have access* to the Father by one Spirit.

From Genesis 12 onwards, when God called Abraham, there has been a difference between the seed of Abraham and the rest of the human race. That division was cemented by the Law of Moses and it can be seen throughout the Old Testament. Not only that, it is still there in the Gospels and even in the book of Acts when, although Gentiles were being saved, the Jews still held first place. All that changed at the end of Acts and Ephesians explains that the Jewish Christians and the Gentile Christians were made one, by God abolishing the Mosaic Law and freeing the Jewish Christians from the need to obey it. This made these two diverse groups one.

So the Law of Moses with its commandments and regulations has been abolished.

Note: Read Colossians 2:13-17 which also states that the Law of Moses, the written code with its regulations, was abolished.

Question: But which commandments and regulations?

Put an X if you think the commandment has been abolished.
Put a tick it you think it is still in operation today.

1. You shall not murder	
2. You shall have no other gods	
3. You shall not use the Lord's name as a swear word	
4. You shall keep the Sabbath Day holy	
5. You shall not commit adultery	
6. You shall circumcise your sons	
7. You shall make a sin offering of a lamb	
8. You shall not steal	
9. You shall not lie	
10.You shall honour your father and mother	
11.You shall fast on the Day of Atonement	
12.You shall not mistreat foreigners	

Answer: Eight still hold true for today. The four which have been abolished are:

1. You shall not murder	
2. You shall have no other gods	
3. You shall not use the Lord's name as a swear word	
4. You shall keep the Sabbath Day holy	X
5. You shall not commit adultery	
6. You shall circumcise your sons	X
7. You shall make a sin offering of a lamb	X

8. You shall not steal	
9. You shall not lie	
10. You shall honour your father and mother	
11. You shall fast on the Day of Atonement	X
12. You shall not mistreat foreigners	

The one which surprises some people is the one relating to the Sabbath day. However, even at the Jerusalem Council in the middle of Acts, when the council debated what Laws the Gentile Christians should observe, keeping of the Sabbath was not one of them. The four rules the Gentiles of that time were given were:

> You are to abstain from food sacrificed to idols, from blood, from the meat of strangled animals and from sexual immorality. You will do well to avoid these things. Farewell. (Acts 15:29)

And after the Law had been abolished we read in Colossians 2:16-17:

> Therefore do not let anyone judge you by what you eat or drink, or with regard to a religious festival, a New Moon celebration or a Sabbath day. These are a shadow of the things that were to come; the reality, however, is found in Christ.

During the Acts the Jewish Christian still had to keep the Sabbath Law. However, now, neither Jewish nor Gentile Christians need observe the Sabbath.

Question: Should Gentiles adhere to the Sabbath principle?

The Sabbath Law declared such things as people could not light fires on the Sabbath. However, the Sabbath principle is that people need one day a week of rest and should come together once a week to worship God; to corporately pray, sing His praises and to be taught about Him. Whether this is on a Saturday or Sunday or Thursday is a side issue.

Task 1. Write down three other laws of Moses which have been abolished.

Task 2. Write down three other laws of Moses which apply today.

Note: If this is being done in a group, compare and discuss answers, but it may be difficult, unless people are well-versed in the Law of Moses and the changes which took place at the end of Acts.

Answer: Generally, the ceremonial, ritualistic, sacrificial laws were abolished. However, the moral and ethical ones still hold and are emphasized in such places as Ephesians chapters 4-6 and Colossians chapters 3 and 4.

Read Colossians 2:13-14.
Fill in the blanks.

When you were dead in your sins and in the uncircumcision of your sinful nature, God made you _ _ _ _ _ with Christ. He forgave us _ _ _ _ _ _ _ _ _ _, having cancelled the written code, with its regulations, that was against us and that stood opposed to us; he took it away, nailing it to the cross.

> When you were dead in your sins and in the uncircumcision of your sinful nature, God made you **alive** with Christ. He forgave us **all our sins**, having cancelled the written code, with its regulations, that was against us and that stood opposed to us; he took it away, nailing it to the cross.

Question: Which of our sins have been forgiven and not remembered?

Answer: All of them.

Question: Which of our sins have been remembered and NOT forgiven?

Answer: None of them.

The BIG Question: SO ... what should our response be to the fact that we were once dead in our sins, *but now* are alive in Christ and once we were Gentiles who were far away, *but now* have been brought close to God?

Ephesians 2:8-10 gives us the general orders.
Fill in the blanks.

For it is by grace you have been saved, through faith - and this is not from yourselves, it is the gift of God - not by works, so that no one can boast. For we are God's workmanship, *created in Christ Jesus _ _ _ _ _ _ _ _ _ _ _ _ _*, which God prepared in advance for us to do.

> For it is by grace you have been saved, through faith - and this is not from yourselves, it is the gift of God - not by works, so that no one can boast. For we are God's workmanship, *created in Christ Jesus* **to do good works**, which God prepared in advance for us to do.

Question: So. what should those 'good works' be?
Ephesians 4:1-3 sets the tone.

As a prisoner for the Lord, then, I urge you to live a life worthy of the calling you have received. (Ephesians 4:1)

Question: What do we have to do to live a life worthy of our calling?

Be completely humble and gentle; be patient, bearing with one another in love. (Ephesians 4:2)

Question: How can we do that?

By making …

.... every effort to keep the unity of the Spirit through the bond of peace. (Ephesians 4:3)

Question: What do we have to do?

Paul's last letter was 2 Timothy and he gave all-embracing advice in 2 Timothy 3:16-17.

All Scripture is God-breathed and is useful for teaching, rebuking, correcting and training in righteousness, so that the man of God may be thoroughly equipped for every good work.

Thus the Bible is the Christian's authority, our guide as to what is right or wrong, as to what we should leave behind and no longer do, and what we should now embrace and do. If we follow the teaching, rebuking, correcting and training given in the Bible we shall be thoroughly equipped for every good work; and we would have found out "what pleases the Lord" (Ephesians 5:10).

Question: However, we have already learnt that the Law of Moses was abolished so how do we know which parts of the Bible we should give a greater emphasis to?

Progressive Revelation

The Bible is a book which unfolds God's plan as we go through it. It contains "Progressive Revelation". So we might find different instructions given to the same people at different times, and we might find different instructions given to different people. That being the case:

Two questions:

Should we give more emphasis to the commands in the earlier parts of the Bible or the later parts?	
Should we give more emphasis to the commands given to Jews or to the ones given to Gentiles?	

Two answers:

Should we give more emphasis to the commands in the earlier parts of the Bible or the later parts?	**Later parts**
Should we give more emphasis to the commands given to Jews or to the ones given to Gentiles?	**Gentiles**

Colossians 3:5-17:

Put to death, therefore, whatever belongs to your earthly nature: sexual immorality, impurity, lust, evil desires and greed, which is idolatry. Because of these, the wrath of God is coming. You used to walk in these ways, in the life you once lived.

But now you must rid yourselves of all such things as these: anger, rage, malice, slander, and filthy language from your lips. Do not lie to each other, since you have taken off your old self with its practices and have put on the new self, which is being renewed in knowledge in the image of its Creator. Here there is no Greek or Jew, circumcised or uncircumcised, barbarian, Scythian, slave or free, but Christ is all, and is in all.

Therefore, as God's chosen people, holy and dearly loved, clothe yourselves with compassion, kindness, humility, gentleness and patience. Bear with each other and forgive whatever grievances you may have against one another. Forgive as the Lord forgave you. And over all these virtues put on love, which binds them all together in perfect unity. Let the peace of Christ rule in your hearts, since as members of one body you were called to peace. And be thankful.

Let the word of Christ dwell in you richly as you teach and admonish one another with all wisdom, and as you sing psalms, hymns and spiritual songs with gratitude in your hearts to God. And whatever you do, whether in word or deed, do it all in the name of the Lord Jesus, giving thanks to God the Father through him.

"Sinning" to "Not Sinning"

The first **'but'** in the study and in Colossians 3:5-17, dealt with the change from what we were as sinners to what we should be in Christ. Put a tick or check mark alongside the things we should do; put an X alongside the things we should not do.

Colossians 3:15-17

Sexual immorality		Slander		Forgiveness	
Impurity		Filthy language		Love	
Lust		Lying		Peace	
Evil desires		Compassion		Thankfulness	
Greed		Kindness		Admonish	
Anger		Humility		Wisdom	
Rage		Gentleness		Song	
Malice		Patience		Gratitude	

Answers: The answers are fairly obvious.

Sexual immorality	X	Slander	X	Forgiveness	/
Impurity	X	Filthy language	X	Love	/
Lust	X	Lying	X	Peace	/
Evil desires	X	Compassion	/	Thankfulness	/
Greed	X	Kindness	/	Admonish	/
Anger	X	Humility	/	Wisdom	/
Rage	X	Gentleness	/	Song	/
Malice	X	Patience	/	Gratitude	/

There is very little change in moral teaching as we progress through the Bible and for most Christians it is not a matter of not knowing what is right or wrong. Rather, it is a matter of doing what is right and not doing what is wrong. This is a problem for us all and Paul also had the same problem 20 or more years after being a Christian. This is what he wrote in Romans 7:18-19.

> I know that nothing good lives in me, that is, in my sinful nature. For I have the desire to do what is good, but I cannot carry it out. For what I do is not the good I want to do; no, the evil I do not want to do - this I keep on doing.

"Law" to "No Law"

The second **'but'** in this study dealt with the change from being Gentiles outside of God's purposes, to being Gentiles who have been brought into them.

New Testament Divisions

Most Christians would automatically give more emphasis to the New Testament than to the Old. However, they can feel uncomfortable about seeing the changes in the New Testament, but they are there. Some changes took place at Pentecost, at the start of the Acts period. There were further changes at the end of the Acts period.

Gospel Period	Acts Period	Post-Acts Period
Almost exclusively Jewish,	*Jews first, but also Gentiles*	*Jew/Gentile - no difference*
Jews under the Law of Moses.	Jewish Christians still under the Law of Moses; Gentile Christians not.	No Christians are under the Law of Moses.
Matthew, Mark, Luke, John	*Letters Written to Jewish Christians* Hebrews, James, 1 & 2 Peter, 1, 2 & 3 John, Jude, Revelation *Letters written to both Jewish and Gentile Christians* Acts, Romans, 1 & 2 Corinthians, Galatians, 1 & 2 Thessalonians	*Letters written to Christians – there being no longer any difference between Jew and Gentile* Ephesians, Philippians, Colossians, 1 & 2 Timothy, Titus, Philemon

Note: Not everything changed at the end of the Acts Period, but some things did and we need to look out for them. As Gentiles we need to give greater emphasis to the teaching of the Post Acts period. All seven were written by Paul who is, in the New Testament, the only person called 'The Apostle to the Gentiles'. These last seven letters contain God's last revelation to mankind. How does this work out in practice?

More examples of Progressive Revelation

The questions in the first column relate to issues which were topical during the Acts Period, but are they relevant today? Yes or no?

The questions in the third column relate to issues written about in the Post-Acts Period. Are they relevant today? Yes or no?

Note: All questions relate to Christians living **today.**

Question	Answer	Question	Answer
Should Christian Jews today circumcise their boy babies in accordance with the Law of Moses?		Should Christian Jews today worry or not about circumcising their boy babies in accordance with Colossians 2:11, 14?	
Should Christian Gentiles today follow the dietary rules issued by the Jerusalem edict in Acts 15:20?		Should Christian Gentiles today worry or not about what they eat in accordance with Colossians 2:16?	
Should Christian Jews today keep all the Sabbath laws laid down in the Law of Moses?		Should Christian Jews today worry or not about keeping the Sabbath in accordance with Colossians 2:14,16?	

Should Christian Gentiles today offer sacrifices for sins in accordance with the Law of Moses?		Should Christian Gentiles today worry or not about animal sacrifices in accordance with Ephesians 2:14-15 and Colossians 2:14?	
Should Christians today expect instant, immediate and complete healing by the laying on of hands?		Should Christians today pray for healing?	
Should Christians today *not* get married, as Paul warned during the Acts Period? (1 Corinthians 7)		Should Christians today get married as Paul advised after the Acts Period? (1 Timothy 5:14)	

Answers:

Question	Answer	Question	Answer
Should Christian Jews today circumcise their boy babies in accordance with the Law of Moses?	NO	Should Christian Jews today worry or not about circumcising their boy babies in accordance with Colossians 2:11, 14?	**NOT WORRY**

Should Christian Gentiles today follow the dietary rules issued by the Jerusalem edict in Acts 15:20?	**NO**	Should Christian Gentiles today worry or not about what they eat in accordance with Colossians 2:16?	**NOT WORRY**
Should Christian Jews today keep all the Sabbath laws laid down in the Law of Moses?	**NO**	Should Christian Jews today worry or not about keeping the Sabbath in accordance with Colossians 2:14,16?	**NOT WORRY**
Should Christian Gentiles today offer sacrifices for sins in accordance with the Law of Moses?	**NO**	Should Christian Gentiles today worry or not about animal sacrifices in accordance with Ephesians 2:14-15 and Colossians 2:14?	**NOT WORRY**
Should Christians today expect instant, immediate and complete healing by the laying on of hands?	**NO**	Should Christians today pray for healing?	**YES**

Should Christians today *not* get married, as Paul warned during the Acts Period? (1 Corinthians 7)	NO	Should Christians today get married as Paul advised after the Acts Period? (1 Timothy 5:14)	YES

Note: If in a group study, compare answers. Again, on subjects such as these, there is likely to be agreement. However, there are some points which may arise.

a) **Circumcision:** there are no Christian reasons for circumcision, although there may be health reasons.

b) **Food:** there are no Christian reasons for not eating any particular food. We need not worry about what meat we eat, or the way in which an animal is killed, provided it is done do so humanely. However, there may be health reasons, such as allergies, for not eating certain foods.

c) **Sabbath Keeping:** there is no statement in the New Testament about Gentiles having to keep the Sabbath. In fact it would be impossible for us to keep all that the Law of Moses says about the Sabbath. However, it may be sensible to follow the Sabbath principle of resting one day in seven and coming together to worship God once a week.

d) **Healing:** in the Acts Period Paul healed freely; we read of no failures. However, after Acts he did not heal Timothy (1 Timothy 5:23), nor Trophimus (2 Timothy 4:20), nor Epaphroditus (Philippians 2:25-28). However, in the last case, Epaphroditus did recover, possibly as a result of prayer.

At the end of Ephesians, Paul sums up what he wants us to do.

The last thing Paul tells Christians to do is in Ephesians 6:10-11: "Finally, be strong in the Lord and in his mighty power."

Question: But how do we do that?
- **How can we be "strong in the Lord"?**
- **How can we be strong "in his mighty power"?**

Answer: By putting on…
The Full Armour of God

Question: Why put on the full Armour of God?
Ephesians 6:11-13.
Fill in the blanks.

Put on the full armour of God … **so that ...**

you can take your _ _ _ _ _ against the devil's schemes. For our struggle is not against _ _ _ _ _ and _ _ _ _ _ but against the _ _ _ _ _ _, against _ _ _ _ _ _ _ _ _ _ _ _ , against the _ _ _ _ _ _ of this dark world and against the _ _ _ _ _ _ _ _ forces of _ _ _ _ in the heavenly realms.

> Put on the full armour of God so that … you can take your stand against the devil's schemes. For our struggle is not against **flesh** and **blood**, but against the **rulers**, against the **authorities**, against the **powers** of this dark world and against the **spiritual** forces of **evil** in the heavenly realms.

Question: We may be able to withstand human attacks, but how can the Christian stand against Satanic ones?

Answer: By putting on put on the full Armour of God.

Ephesians 6:13-18

Fill in the blanks.

Put on the full armour of God … **so that …**

when the day of evil comes, you may be able to _ _ _ _ _ your ground, and after you have done everything, to _ _ _ _ _. _ _ _ _ _ _ firm then, with the _ _ _ _ of truth buckled around your waist, with the _ _ _ _ _ _ _ _ _ _ _ of righteousness in place, and with your feet fitted with the readiness that comes from the gospel of peace. In addition to all this, take up the _ _ _ _ _ _ of faith, with which you can extinguish all the flaming arrows of the evil one. Take the _ _ _ _ _ _ of salvation and the _ _ _ _ _ of the Spirit, which is the _ _ _ _ of God.

> Put on the full armour of God so that … when the day of evil comes, you may be able to **stand** your ground, and after you have done everything, to **stand**. **Stand** firm then, with the **belt** of truth buckled round your waist, with the **breastplate** of righteousness in place, and with your feet fitted with the readiness that comes from the gospel of peace. In addition to all this, take up the **shield** of faith, with which you can extinguish all the flaming arrows of the evil one. Take the **helmet** of salvation and the **sword** of the Spirit, which is the **word** of God.

Notice the three-fold order to 'Stand'.

1) when the day of evil comes, you may be able to **stand** your ground,
2) and after you have done everything, to **stand**.
3) **Stand** firm then

This is not an attack with the aim of gaining ground; it is a command to stand firm and not give any ground. When a Roman legion went into defensive formation, they were very difficult to defeat.

Note also that the only attacking weapon is "the **sword** of the Spirit, which is the **word of God**". It is imperative that Christians know what the Bible says and understand it and appreciate progressive revelation.

And Pray

Ephesians 6:18.
Fill in the blanks.

_ _ _ _ in the Spirit on all occasions with all kinds of _ _ _ _ _ _ _ and requests. With this in mind, be alert and always keep on
_ _ _ _ _ _ _ for all the saints.

> **Pray** in the Spirit on all occasions with all kinds of **prayers** and requests. With this in mind, be alert and always keep on **praying** for all the saints.

Note the importance of prayer. However, prayer is never described as a weapon in the Bible. The only weapon is the Bible. I have often heard it said that today's churches are struggling or failing because there is not enough prayer; there is certainly far more prayer than there is Bible study. Our churches may be struggling and failing because the Christians in them do not know the Bible and so are not able to carry out Peter's command and Paul's desire..

> Always be prepared to give an answer to everyone who asks you to give the reason for the hope that you have. (1 Peter 3:15)

Be wise in the way you act toward outsiders; make the most of every opportunity. Let your conversation be always full of grace, seasoned with salt, so that you may know how to answer everyone. (Colossians 4:5-6)

Don't forget to pray.

Prayer is important and, by and large the vast majority of Christians pray. They probably pray far more than they read and study their Bible.

So don't forget to read and study the Bible ...

Not only do we have to read the Bible, we need to believe it. That does not mean to say we think that everything is relevant to us Gentiles living today. However, we should do what it states that Gentiles should do, especially what is made clear in the last seven letters of Paul. If we do that, then life will better for us personally and also for society.

Balance:
Blessings and Response:
Part 1

Getting the balance right
Blessings and response

We were once dead in our sins,
but now God has made us alive in Christ,

THEREFORE

We should live a life worth of our calling
by not doing the things that are wrong,
but rather doing those which are right.

We have been saved by grace through faith, not of works, so that no one can boast. However, we have been saved *for* good works which God wants us to do, and those good works are recorded in the Bible; the do's and don'ts; the rights and wrongs.

Balance:
Blessings and Response:
Part 2

Getting the balance right
Blessings and response

Once we were Gentiles who were far away,
but now have been brought close to God,

THEREFORE

We should do the things
that God wants Gentiles to do,
rather than those things
He wanted from the Jews.

We are Gentiles who have been brought into God's plan. Therefore we should live the life that God wants Gentiles to live today, not the one He wanted Jews to live in the past.

****

****

About the author

Michael Penny was born in Ebbw Vale, Gwent, Wales in 1943. He read Mathematics at the University of Reading, before teaching for twelve years and becoming the Director of Mathematics and Business Studies at Queen Mary's College Basingstoke in Hampshire, England. In 1978 he entered Christian publishing, and in 1984 became the administrator of the Open Bible Trust.

He held this position for seven years, before moving to the USA and becoming pastor of Grace Church in New Berlin, Wisconsin. He returned to Britain in 1999, and is at present the Administrator and Editor of The Open Bible Trust. In 2010 he was elected Chairman of Churches Together in Reading, where he speaks in a number of churches. He is a member of the Advisory Committee to Reading University Christian Union and is a chaplain at Reading College, and has helped set up chaplaincy teams in a number of other colleges.

He lives near Reading with his wife and has appeared on BBC Radio Berkshire and Premier Radio a number of times. He has made several speaking tours of America, Canada, Australia, New Zealand and the Netherlands, as well as ones to South Africa and the Philippines. Some of his writings have been translated into German and Russian.

As well as editing and writing articles for *Search* magazine and many Bible study booklets, he has also written several major books including: *The Manual on the Gospel of John; 40 Problem Passages; Approaching the Bible; The Bible! Myth or Message?; Galatians - Interpretation and Application; The Miracles of the Apostles; Introducing God's Word* (with Carol Brown and Lynn Mrotek); *Introducing God's Plan* (with Sylvia Penny).

He has written two books with W M Henry

- *Following Philippians*, which is ideal for Post-Alpha groups
- *The Will of God: Past and Present.*

His latest books are:

- *Joel's Prophecy: Past and Future*
- *James; His Life and Letter*
- *Paul: A Missionary of Genius*
- *Peter: His life and letters*
- *John: His life and writings*

Details of these books, and other writings, can be seen at

www.obt.org.uk

****

Michael Penny is editor of *Search* magazine

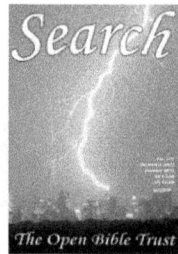

For a free sample of
The Open Bible Trust's magazine *Search*,
please email

admin@obt.org.uk

or visit

www.obt.org.uk/search

Also by Michael Penny

If you have enjoyed *The Balanced Christian Life* you may like to read the *Manual on the Gospel of John.*

This book is a 'manual' in the sense that it requires 'work' on the part of the reader. The book is in the following format.

Manual on the Gospel of John

Michael Penny

- First, a passage from John's Gospel is reproduced.
- Then follows a series of question on that passage.
- After each question a 'hint' is given in case the reader has difficulty in answering the question.
- Then the author's answer is given.

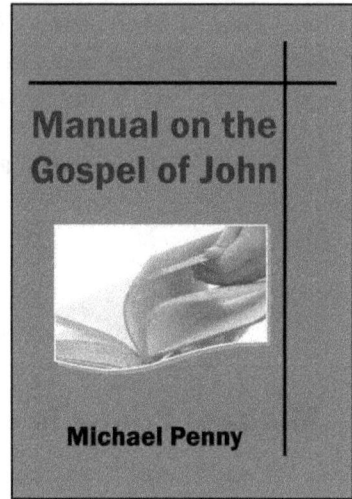

The desire of the author is for the reader to answer the question before going on to read his suggested answer.

*****

For further details of this book, and the ones on the next pages, please visit **www.obt.org.uk**

These books can be ordered from that website and also from

The Open Bible Trust
Fordland Mount, Upper Basildon,
Reading, RG8 8LU, UK.

They are also available as eBooks from Amazon and Apple and as KDP paperbacks from Amazon.

True or False?
Comments and Queries about The New Testament
By Michael Penny

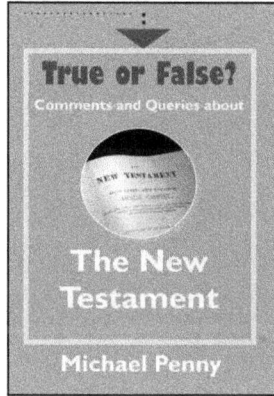

Are these True or False?

- People need faith to be healed
- The Kingdom of God is within you
- The Great Commission is our commission
- Paul should have replaced Judas
- Pentecost is the *birthday* of the Church
- Confession is a 'must' for forgiveness
- Whoever is born of God does not sin
- Paul was against marriage
- The New Covenant belongs to Gentiles
- Prayer is a weapon
- Women should not teach men

These and twenty other comments and queries are discussed in a thought provoking manner. The aim of the author is to encourage people to 'think' about what they hear and read, and about what they believe. Which of the above are true? Which are false?

True or False?

Comments and Queries about Christianity

by Michael Penny

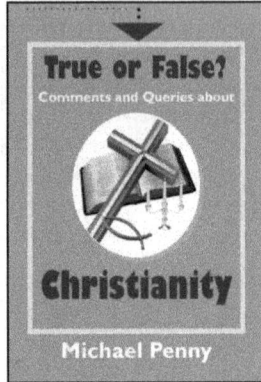

Are these True or False?

- This is the best of all possible worlds.
- Christians should practise what they preach.
- Heaven is perfect.
- The Kingdom is extended by kindness
- Sexual morals are out of date.
- It is impossible to know God.
- Suffering shows there is no God.
- God calls us home.
- We should do what Jesus would do.
- Christ condoned adultery.
- The Holy Spirit can be taken from us.

These and twenty other comments and queries are discussed in a thought provoking manner. The aim of the author is to encourage people to 'think' about what they hear and read, and about what they believe. Which of the above are true? Which are false?

About this book

The Balanced Christian Life

This is a series of five detailed studies based on Ephesians exploring the blessings Christians have in Christ and explaining the practical Christian life which should follow.

Its format is interactive with many questions and tasks, which the reader is asked to answer and consider (or if in a group to discuss) before looking at the author's answer.

This is an excellent introduction to Paul's letters to the Ephesians.

****